D0578632

8/02

First published in the UK by Scholastic Publications Ltd, 1993.

Library of Congress Cataloging-in-Publication Data

Cowcher, Helen.
    Whistling thorn / Helen Cowcher.
        p.   cm.
    Summary: Explains how the acacia evolved its own protection
against browsing animals and helped create a balanced natural
environment.
    ISBN 0-590-47299-2
    l. Acacia — Africa — Evolution — Juvenile literature.   2. Acacia —
Africa — Ecology — Juvenile literature.   [1. Acacia.   2. Ecology —
Africa.]   I. Title.
QK495.M545C68 1993   92-39533
583'.321 — dc20   CIP
                                                          AC

12 11 10 9 8 7 6 5 4 3 2 1   3 4 5 6 7 8/9

Printed in Hong Kong

First Scholastic printing, October 1993

For the paintings in this book,
the illustrator used watercolor and gouache.

In this book, the term *gall* refers to the swollen growth
at the base of the thorns on African acacia bushes.

WHISTLING THORN

HELEN COWCHER

SCHOLASTIC
HARDCOVER

SCHOLASTIC INC. / New York

Long ago, on the grasslands of Africa,
there grew acacia bushes.
They were the favorite food
of giraffes and rhinos.

Giraffe stretched out his long tongue
and grasped the juicy rich leaves.
Rhino nibbled contentedly.
The bushes were many . . .

... but so, in those far-off days,

were the giraffes and rhinos.

Even the tiniest acacia buds were eaten.

Rhino, like all his fellow rhinos,
rested for hours in the shade,
each day,

and only wandered to the acacias
when he felt very hungry.
The rhinos never ate at any bush
long enough to do real harm.

But the giraffes ate constantly.
They could reach even the highest branches,
taking far too much from each bush.

As time passed, the acacias grew
sharp thorns, some shaped like galls.
Ants smelled sweet acacia nectar
and came to make their nests.

They made entrance holes in the galls.

When the wind came blowing across the savannah,

it piped through the holes

like the music of a thousand flutes.

The sound of WHISTLING THORNS!

One day, a hungry giraffe

was tugging at the acacia shoots,

relentlessly shaking the thorny branches . . .

. . . rocking the galls.

Frenzied ants scrambled from their homes,

crawling in a steady stream
over the giraffe's muzzle,
stinging as they went.

They climbed around the giraffe's eye ...

... irritating him so much that he
could stand it no longer.
He moved on,
shaking the ants free.

The same fate awaited each giraffe;
one by one, spurred on
by stinging ants,
they moved quickly to other
whistling thorn bushes.

Now the bushes had time to grow fresh leaves,
while the giraffes and rhinos could still
eat their favorite food.
A warm breeze washed over them
as they grazed under the
hot savannah sun, and flute music
flowed from the whistling thorns.